I dedicate this book to my wife, Jess, and our children Chiara and Daniel.
Thank you for the love and support.

ISBN (Paperback) 978-1-955364-32-4
ISBN (Ebook) 978-1-955364-35-5
Vets Publish
www.vetspublish.com

AMHARIC

AMHARIC HAS 57 MILLION SPEAKERS

Amharic is the most widely spoken language in Ethiopia.

Number	Written	Spoken
0	ዜሮ	zēro
1	አንድ	ānidi
2	ሁለት	huleti
3	ሶስት	sositi
4	አራት	ārati
5	አምስc	āmisiti
6	ስድስት	sidisiti
7	ሰባት	sebati
8	ስምት	simiti
9	ዘጠኝ	zet'enyi
10	አስc	āsiri

Saying Hello	ሠላም-šelami

BENGALI

BENGALI HAS 300 MILLION SPEAKERS

Bengali is the national language of Bangladesh.

Number	Written	Spoken
0	শূন্য	Śūn'ya
1	এক	Ēka
2	দুই	du'I
3	তিন	tina
4	চার	cāra
5	পাঁচ	pām̐ca
6	ছয়	chaẏa
7	সাত	sāta
8	আট	āṭa
9	নয়টি	naẏaṭi
10	দশ	daśa

Saying Hello   নমস্কার - Namaskāra

CHICHEWA
CHICEWA HAS 1 MILLION SPEAKERS
Chichewa is a Bantu language spoken in Malawi.

Number	Written and Spoken
0	ziro
1	imodzi
2	awiri
3	atatu
4	zinayi
5	zisanu
6	zisanu ndi chimodzi
7	Zisanu ndi ziwiri
8	eyiti
9	zisanu ndi zinayi
10	khumi

Saying Hello	Moni

DUTCH

DUTCH HAS 30 MILLION SPEAKERS

Dutch is the primary language of the Netherlands.

Number	Written and Spoken
0	Nul
1	Een
2	Twee
3	Drie
4	vier
5	Vijf
6	Zes
7	zeven
8	acht
9	negen
10	tien

Saying Hello	Hallo

ENGLISH

ENGLISH HAS 1 BILLION SPEAKERS

English is the primary language of the United States of America, Canada, The United Kingdom, Australia and many other nations.

Number	Written and Spoken
0	Zero
1	One
2	Two
3	Three
4	Four
5	Five
6	Six
7	Seven
8	Eight
9	Nine
10	Ten
Saying Hello	Hello

FRENCH

FRENCH HAS 270 MILLION SPEAKERS

French is the primary language of 29 countries.

Number	Written and Spoken
0	Zéro
1	Un
2	Deux
3	Trois
4	Quatre
5	Cinq
6	Six
7	Sept
8	huit
9	neuf
10	Dix

Saying Hello	Bonjour

GUJARATI
GUJARATI HAS 56.4 MILLION SPEAKERS
Gujarati is the 6th most common language in India. It is also the official language in the state of Gujarat.

Number	Written	Spoken
0	શૂન્ય	Śūn'ya
1	એક	ēka
2	બે	bē
3	ત્રણ	traṇa
4	ચાર	cāra
5	પાંચ	pāñca
6	છ	cha
7	સાત	sāta
8	આઠ	āṭha
9	નવ	nava
10	દસ	dasa

Saying Hello	Namastē

HAUSA

HAUSA HAS 72 MILLION SPEAKERS

Spoken by the Hausa people in the northern half of Nigeria, Ghana, Cameroon, Benin and Togo, and the southern half of Niger, Chad and South Sudan, with significant minorities in Ivory Coast.

Number	Written and Spoken
0	Sifili
1	Daya
2	Biyu
3	Uku
4	Hudu
5	Biyar
6	Shida
7	Bakwai
8	takwas
9	tara
10	goma

Saying Hello	Sannu

ITALIAN
ITALIAN HAS 65 MILLION SPEAKERS
Italian is the primary language in Italy.

Number	Written and Spoken
0	zero
1	uno
2	Due
3	tre
4	quattro
5	cinque
6	sei
7	Sette
8	otto
9	nove
10	dieci

Saying Hello	Ciao

JAPANESE

JAPANESE HAS 128 MILLION SPEAKERS

Japanese has several writing systems: kanji 漢字, hiragana ひらがな or 平仮名 and katakana カタカナ or 片仮名.

Number	Written	Spoken
0	れい、ぜろ	rei, zero
1	いち	ichi
2	に	ni
3	さん	san
4	し、よん	shi, yon
5	ご	go
6	ろく	roku
7	しち、なな	shichi, nana
8	はち	hachi
9	きゅう、く	kyuu, ku
10	じゅう	juu

Saying Hello	Kon'nichiwa

KOREAN

KOREAN HAS 80 MILLION SPEAKERS

Korean is the native language of North Korea and South Korea.

Number	Written	Spoken
0	영	yeong
1	하나	hana
2	둘	dul
3	셋	set
4	넷	net
5	다섯	daseot
6	여섯	yeoseot
7	일곱	ilgop
8	여덟	yeodeol
9	아홉	ahop
10	열	yeol

Saying Hello   안녕하세요   **An yeong ha se yo**

LINGALA

LINGALA HAS 20 MILLION SPEAKERS

Lingala is a Bantu language spoken in The Democratic Republic of the Congo and The Republic of the Congo.

Number	Written and Spoken
0	libungutulu
1	moko
2	mibale
3	misato
4	minei
5	mitano
6	motoba
7	nsambo
8	mwambe
9	libwa
10	zomi
Saying Hello	**Mbote**

MANDARIN

MANDARIN HAS OVER 1 BILLION SPEAKERS

Mandarin is the official language of China, Singapore, and Taiwan.

Number	Written	Spoken
0	零	Líng
1	一	yī
2	二	èr
3	三	sān
4	四	sì
5	五	wǔ
6	六	liù
7	七	qī
8	八	bā
9	九	jiǔ
10	十	shí

Saying Hello	你好	Nǐ hǎo

NAPALI

NAPALI HAS OVER 20 MILLION SPEAKERS

Napali is the main language of Nepal.

Number	Written	Spoken
0	शून्य	Śūn'ya
1	एउटा	ē'uṭā
2	दुई	du'ī
3	तीन	tīna
4	चार	cāra
5	पाँच	pām̐ca
6	छ	cha
7	सात	sāta
8	आठ	āṭha
9	नौ	nau
10	दस	dasa

Saying Hello	नमस्कार	Namaskāra

OROMO

OROMO HAS 20 MILLION SPEAKERS

Oromo has the largest number of native speakers in Ethiopia.
It also has native speakers in Kenya.

Number	Written and Spoken
0	zeeroo
1	tokko
2	lama
3	sadii
4	afur
5	shan
6	ja'a
7	torba
8	saddeet
9	sagal
10	kudhan

Saying Hello	Akkam

POLISH

POLISH HAS 20 MILLION SPEAKERS

The traditional 32-letter Polish alphabet has nine additions (ą, ć, ę, ł, ń, ó, ś, ź, ż) to the letters of the basic 26-letter Latin alphabet, while removing three (x, q, v).

Number	Written and Spoken
0	zero
1	jeden
2	dwa
3	trzy
4	cztery
5	pięć
6	sześć
7	siedem
8	osiem
9	dziewięć
10	dziesięć

Saying Hello	Witam

QUECHUA
QUECHUA HAS 7 MILLION SPEAKERS

Quechua is an indigenous language family spoken by the Quechua peoples, primarily living in the Peruvian Andes.

Number	Written and Spoken
0	chusaq
1	huk
2	iskay
3	kimsa
4	tawa
5	pichqa
6	suqta
7	qanchis
8	pasuq
9	isqun
10	chunka

Saying Hello	Allinllachu

RUSSIAN

RUSSIAN HAS OVER 258 MILLION SPEAKERS

Besides Russia itself, Russian is an official language in Belarus, Kazakhstan, and Kyrgyzstan,.

Number	Written	Spoken
0	нуль	nul'
1	один	odin
2	два	dva
3	три	tri
4	четыре	chetyre
5	пять	piat'
6	шесть	shest'
7	Семь	Sem'
8	восемь	vosem'
9	девять	devyat'
10	десять	desiat'

Saying Hello привет privet

SPANISH

SPANISH HAS 500 MILLION SPEAKERS

Spanish is the official language of 20 countries.

Number	Written and Spoken
0	cero
1	uno
2	dos
3	tres
4	cuatro
5	cinco
6	seis
7	siete
8	ocho
9	nueve
10	diez

Saying Hello	Hola

THAI
THAI HAS OVER 60 MILLION SPEAKERS
It is also a minority language in Cambodia, Laos, Malaysia, and Myanmar.

Number	Written	Spoken
0	ศูนย์	s̄ūný
1	หนึ่ง	h̄nụ̀ng
2	สอง	s̄xng
3	สาม	s̄ām
4	สี่	s̄ī̀
5	ห้า	h̄̂ā
6	หก	h̄k
7	เจ็ด	se wèn
8	แปด	pæd
9	เก้า	kêā
10	สิบ	s̄ib

Saying Hello	สวัสดี	Sawasdee

UKRAINIAN

UKRAINIAN HAS OVER 27 MILLION SPEAKERS

Comparisons are often drawn to Russian, another East Slavic language, but there is more mutual intelligibility with Belarusian.

Number	Written	Spoken
0	нуль	nul'
1	один	odyn
2	два	dva
3	три	try
4	чотири	chotyry
5	п'ять	p'yat'
6	шість	shist'
7	сім	sim
8	вісім	visim
9	дев'ять	dev'yat'
10	десять	desyat'

Saying Hello	привіт	pryvit

VIETNAMESE

VIETNAMESE HAS OVER 70 MILLION SPEAKERS

Vietnamese is a minority language In Cambodia, Czech Republican, and Laos.

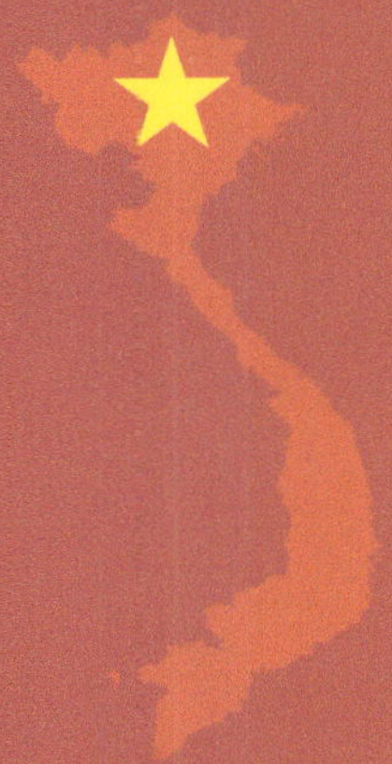

Number	Written	Spoken
0	không	Kong
1	một	moat
2	hai	hi
3	ba	bath
4	bốn	bone
5	năm	nahm
6	sáu	saow
7	bảy	bayh
8	tám	tahm
9	chín	cheen
10	mười	muhey
Saying Hello	chào	chow

WELSH

WELSH HAS 500 THOUSAND SPEAKERS

Welsh is spoken natively in Wales, by some in England, and
in Y Wladfa, a Welsh colony in Chubut Province, Argentina.

Number	Written and Spoken
0	sero
1	un
2	dwy
3	tri
4	pedwar
5	pump
6	chwech
7	saith
8	wyth
9	naw
10	deg

Saying Hello	Helo

XHOSA

XHOSA HAS 20 MILLION SPEAKERS

Xhosa is one of the official languages of both South Africa and Zimbabwe.

Number	Written and Spoken
0	unothi
1	nye
2	mbini
3	ntathu
4	ezine
5	ntlanu
6	ntandathu
7	sixhengxe
8	sibhozo
9	thoba
10	shumi

yibambe = hold strong

Saying Hello	Molo

YIDDISH

YIDDISH HAS ONLY 600 THOUSAND SPEAKERS

It originates from 9th century based on High German fused with many elements taken from Hebrew and to some extent Aramaic.

Number	Written	Spoken
0	נול	nul
1	איינער	eyner
2	צוויי	tsvey
3	דרײַ	dray
4	פיר	fir
5	פינף	finf
6	זעקס	zex
7	זיבן	zibn
8	אַכט	akht
9	ניין	neyn
10	צען	tsen

Saying Hello	העלא hela

ZULU

ZULU HAS 12 MILLION SPEAKERS

Zulu is the most widely spoken home language in South Africa. The Zulu language possesses several click sounds typical of Southern African languages, not found in the rest of Africa.

Number	Written and Spoken
0	uziro
1	eyodwa
2	ezimbili
3	ezintathu
4	ezine
5	amahlanu
6	eziyisithupha
7	Isikhombisa
8	ayisishiyagalombili
9	ayisishiyagalolunye
10	eziyishumi
Saying Hello	Sawubona

Thank you for reading the ABC's of Languages for Kids.

Please consider leaving a review on Amazon, Goodreads or your site of choice.